Three Interlu[des]

for E♭/B♭ saxophone with piano

für Saxophone in B oder Es und Klavier

pour saxophone alto ou ténor et piano

MICHAEL HENRY

ALTO SAXOPHONE (E♭)

TENOR SAXOPHONE (B♭)

(Interlude 3 is intended for E♭ saxophone only)

FABER *ff* MUSIC

Interlude 1

Michael Henry

Interlude 2

Michael Henry

* 8ve ad lib.

Interlude 3

Michael Henry

Interlude 1

Michael Henry

Interlude 2

Michael Henry

* 8ve ad lib.

Three Interludes

for Eb/Bb saxophone with piano

für Saxophone in B oder Es und Klavier

pour saxophone alto ou ténor et piano

MICHAEL HENRY

Contents

These three short interludes progress in difficulty and may be played either separately as exam/study pieces, or together as a short concert suite.

Michael Henry studied composition at the Royal College of Music, London; he has won the Joseph Horovitz, Stanford and Cornelius Cardew prizes for composition and has had several works broadcast by BBC Radio 3. He plays saxophone and clarinet in a variety of ensembles including rhythm & blues and rock bands, and sings with *The Flying Pickets* and various soul groups. As a high-baritone he specialises in contemporary opera and has performed at Glyndebourne and other major operatic venues.

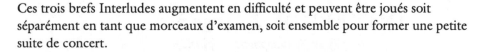

Diese drei kurzen Zwischenspiele sind in fortschreitendem Schwierigkeitsgrad geschrieben. Sie können entweder einzeln als Prüfungs- oder Studienwerke oder aber zusammenhängend als kleine Konzertsuite gespielt werden.

Michael Henry studierte Komposition am Royal College of Music in London. Er ist Träger zweier Kompositionspreise (Joseph Horovitz, Stanford und Cornelius Cardew); mehrere seiner Werke sind von BBC Radio 3 gesendet worden. Er spielt in verschiedenen Ensembles Saxophon und Klarinette, darunter Rhythm & Blues und Rock Bands. Außerdem ist er Sänger bei den *Flying Pickets* und bei verschiedenen anderen Soul-Gruppen. Als hoher Bariton hat er sich auf die zeitgenössische Oper spezialisiert und ist in Glyndebourne und bei anderen wichtigen Opernunternehmungen aufgetreten.

Ces trois brefs Interludes augmentent en difficulté et peuvent être joués soit séparément en tant que morceaux d'examen, soit ensemble pour former une petite suite de concert.

Michael Henry a étudié la composition au Royal College of Music de Londres. Il a obtenu les prix de composition Joseph Horowitz, Stanford et Cornelius Cardew, et BBC Radio 3 a diffusé plusieurs de ses oeuvres. Il joue du saxophone et de la clarinette dans plusieurs ensembles, dont des groupes de 'rhythm and blues' et de rock, et il chante au sein des *Flying Pickets* comme d'autres formations de musique soul. Baryton aigu, il se spécialise dans l'opéra contemporain et s'est produit à Glyndebourne ainsi que sur d'autres grandes scènes d'opéra.

© 1995 by Faber Music Ltd
First published in 1995 by Faber Music Ltd
3 Queen Square London WC1N 3AU
Cover design by S & M Tucker
Music processed by Donald Sheppard
Printed in England by Halstan & Co Ltd
All rights reserved

ISBN 0 571 51541 X

Interlude 1

Michael Henry

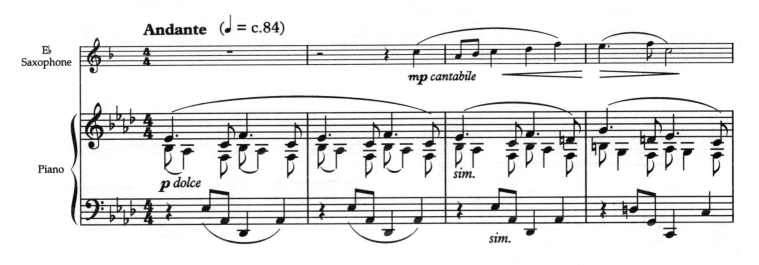

Interlude 2

Michael Henry

* 8ve ad lib.

Interlude 3

Michael Henry